I0419456

Quote Octopus
Melbourne, Victoria, 3053
Australia
www.quoteoctopus.com

Plagiarism has been around far longer than the Internet. In fact, I had a poem published in 'Seventeen' magazine when I was 15 years old. About a year later I was informed that there was a girl who used that same poem to win a statewide poetry competition in Alabama. It took months for people to put together that this had happened.

Megan McCafferty

My daddy wanted me to be a farmer; feel the smoothness of Alabama clay and become one of the first blacks in my town to own land. But, I was worried about my history being caked with that southern clay, and I subscribed to a different kind of teaching and learning in my bones and in my spirit.

John Henrik Clarke

As the eldest son of an Alabama sharecropper family, I was constantly troubled by a collage of North American southern behaviors and notions in reference to the inhumanity of people. There were questions that I did not know how to ask but could, in my young, unsophisticated way, articulate a series of answers.

John Henrik Clarke

I know my destiny. I was born into animosity, bigotry and hatred. We had water for white folks, and water for coloured folks. White lines, black lines. I came from Beaufort in South Carolina, and it was tougher than Georgia, Alabama and Mississippi.

Joe Frazier

My grandmother was born in 1900, and she would regale me with tales I call 'Little House on the Prairie' tales, but they were tales of segregated and racist America growing up in Alabama and Mississippi, where she came from.

David Alan Grier

Some of you may know my story: How for nineteen years, I worked as a manager for a tire plant in Alabama. And some of you may have lived a similar story: After nearly two decades of hard, proud work, I found out that I was making significantly less money than the men who were doing the same work as me.

Lilly Ledbetter

Only when Christ comes again will the little white children of Alabama walk hand in hand with little black children.

Billy Graham

By and large, the making of motion pictures is all about, 'Let's ratchet it up.' And I always think, 'We don't need to ratchet this up.' If you do, don't call it 'Captain Phillips' or 'The Maersk Alabama.' Call it something else, and then you have carte blanche to do anything, down to sea serpents and aliens.

Tom Hanks

I grew up in Mobile, Alabama - somebody's got to be from Mobile, right? - and Mobile sits at the confluence of five rivers, forming this beautiful delta. And the delta has alligators crawling in and out of rivers filled with fish and cypress trees dripping with snakes, birds of every flavor.

Mike deGruy

So in my freshman year at the University of Alabama, learning the literature on evolution, what was known about it biologically, just gradually transformed me by taking me out of literalism and increasingly into a more secular, scientific view of the world.

E. O. Wilson

People in north Michigan are not different at all from people in southern Alabama. Trust me, someone who's spent a lot of time in both places. They're all hardworking, simple people.

Kid Rock

Hollywood is run by people who sit up in their executive office, who are not connected to Mississippi, Alabama, Chicago, South Carolina. They know nothing about that, they don't go to church, and they make their decisions about what they think is right.

Steve Harvey

I plan on staying at Alabama for the rest of my career. I guarantee that I'll be here for you through it all, regardless of what happens.

Bear Bryant

I make a lot of money. I can take a pay cut. All my friends are taking pay cuts that are in the unions, that are - that are farming in Alabama or whatever it is. I can surely take a pay cut, too, not cutting down my show or - or the people that work for me, I can take a pay cut.

Kid Rock

I love what Alabama Shakes is doing - it's kind of like what grunge did to rock 'n' roll, they're doing to R&B.

John Oates

By growing up in Alabama, I had a melting pot of the whole pie: R&B, gospel, country.

Lionel Richie

When cyclones tear up Oklahoma and hurricanes swamp Alabama and wildfires scorch Texas, you come to us, the rest of the country, for billions of dollars to recover. And the damage that your polluters and deniers are doing doesn't just hit Oklahoma and Alabama and Texas. It hits Rhode Island with floods and storms.

Sheldon Whitehouse

You can talk about teamwork on a baseball team, but I'll tell you, it takes teamwork when you have 2,900 men stationed on the U.S.S. Alabama in the South Pacific.

Bob Feller

I've had many a player tell me all through high school and right up until signing day that they were coming to Alabama, then they signed with somebody else.

Bear Bryant

I was only a gun captain on the battleship Alabama for 34 months. People have called me a hero for that, but I'll tell you this - heroes don't come home. Survivors come home.

Bob Feller

As far as heroes thorough the years, I'd say definitely Alabama and Randy Owen, Conway Twitty was a big influence of mine, George Strait, Lionel Richie.

Luke Bryan

Like all soul singers, I grew up singing in church but sometimes I would leave early and sit in the car listening to gospel band, The Blind Boys of Alabama. Hearing their lead singer Clarence made me connect the idea of church and show business and see how I could make a career singing music that stirred the soul.

Daryl Hall

Alabama seniors all across the Third Congressional District continue facing high drug costs.

Mike Rogers

Alabama - they were the masters of that. They could come out with 'Mountain Music' or 'Tennessee River' and then turn around and come out with 'Feels So Right.' Go out and have fun and be those guys that like to party, then turn around and make every woman in America want Randy Owen.

Jason Aldean

The worst gig story I have is from a club in Alabama that I think is still up and running, so I won't name the name of the club. We got hired in there to play, and the owner was pretty annoying. He kept coming up to me during the show and asking me to play 'Purple Rain.'

Jason Aldean

The saddest face I ever saw on Martin Luther King was at the funeral of the four little girls slain in Birmingham, Alabama.

James A. Forbes

I think of myself as a Hollywood hillbilly, but I'm sick of all these questions people ask about Alabama. 'Do you have an outhouse?' 'Is there a lot of inbreeding in your family?' They think all Southerners don't have computers and TV sets and that we're all still living in 1862.

Sunny Mabrey

I used to play too with a boy who played a saxophone. We didn't play no blues, we'd play a lot of love songs - 'Stardust', 'Blue Moon', 'Out Cold Again', 'Sophisticated Lady', 'Stars Fell On Alabama', a lot of different stuff.

David Edwards

I grew up in a rural area. I grew up in deep southern middle Tennessee, probably about thirty miles from the Alabama border. There's nothing there, really. And the TV was my link to the outside world. It's what kept me from going into factory employment. It's what made me want to go to college. It was really inspiring.

DJ Qualls

I'm from Alabama and I have morals and I have class. That's my personality.

Katherine Webb

I don't do Jewish stuff because I don't want people to be left out. If I mention the Torah in Alabama, it's not going to go down that well. I used to do some Jewish jokes because when I started, I used to play lots of Jewish country clubs.

Rita Rudner

I got the chance to argue my first case in Supreme Court, a criminal case arising in Alabama that involved the right of a defendant to counsel at a critical stage in a capital case before a trial.

Constance Baker Motley

I got the sense that Alabama is a place where people don't want handouts and don't much care for people talking out of the side of their mouth.

Adam McKay

I was born in Alabama, but I only lived there for a month before I'd done everything there was to do.

Paula Poundstone

The great thing that I appreciate - the fact that my godfather, William 'Sticky' Jackson, was a Tuskegee Airman because my father was first born in Ozark, Alabama. The sacrifices and the commitment of those men made it possible for myself and many others.

Allen West

I spent 34 months on the battleship Alabama, South Dakota-class. I was a gun captain. First we went to Russia for about 11 months with the British convoys. Then we were up in Norway and Scandinavia.

Bob Feller

However, before we make the mistake of patting ourselves on the back, let's remember: government does not create jobs. It only helps create the conditions that make jobs more or less likely. The real credit for our economic renewal belongs to the people of Alabama .

Bob Riley

I was born in Alabama and my first live music experiences were in church. Every Sunday we watched regional gospel groups on television singing their hearts out.

Tommy Shaw

People who have not done their research on me do not know that I am European, born in Copenhagen, Denmark to an Italian father from Napoli and a mother from Alabama who was singing opera and went to Europe, met my dad, fell in love, and then moved back to Rome, where I was raised, between Rome and Hamburg.

Giancarlo Esposito

I played the young Reese Witherspoon in 'Sweet Home Alabama' when I was 7, and the boy who played the young Josh Lucas was 10.

Dakota Fanning

Oscar Charleston was the Willie Mays of his day. Nobody ever played center field better than Willie Mays. Suppose they had never given Willie a chance, and we said that, would anybody believe there was a kid in Alabama who was that good? Or there was a black guy in Atlanta who might break Babe Ruth's home run record? No.

Monte Irvin

I was raised in South Alabama in the woods, y'know? I'm country.

Shelby Lynne

The repeal of racist language in the Constitution of Alabama was and still is a necessary step in the state's ability to progress.

Artur Davis

While the level of support we can each provide certainly varies, it is very important at this time that we all do what we can to help our neighbors - not only our immediate neighbors here in Alabama, but those further away in Mississippi and Louisiana.

Jo Bonner

He wants to be his own man and be recognized for what he's done. He's not asking for anything because of his name. That was a tough situation to go into at Alabama, but he probably wouldn't have been given the job if the situation would have been different.

Don Shula

It is my belief CAFTA will be beneficial for Alabama and the United States as a whole.

Spencer Bachus

The combat environment has the effect of flattening out civilian identities. If you're young or old, or a graduate from Harvard or the son of a farmer from Alabama, or if you're gay or straight or good-looking or ugly: none of those things matters much in combat, as long as you can conform to the group expectations.

Sebastian Junger

We're given the springboard of the text, a plane ticket, told to report to Alabama, and there's a group of people all ready to make a film and it's a marvelous life.

Albert Finney

My mother was a leading lady in a local theatre in Birmingham, Alabama, where I grew up.

Mary Badham

We have built a genuine level of enthusiasm and goodwill with people throughout this district. People are really excited about the possibilities this election holds, not just for this district, but because of the message Alabama sent to the rest of the country.

Artur Davis

If you are a gay couple living in Alabama, you know one thing: your family has no standing under the law; and it can and will be violated by strangers.

Andrew Sullivan

When I was on 'All My Children,' we did a thing for 'Seventeen Magazine' where a girl won a date. I went to her prom with her in Alabama, and she was a sweetheart. I didn't move to Alabama and I didn't buy a farm there, but we still keep in touch.

Josh Duhamel

I never apologize for my efforts to support worthy projects that Alabama.

Richard Shelby

I firmly believe a rising tide lifts all boats. I think having Airbus only grows and brings more attention to Alabama's entire aerospace and aviation industry. Listen, my goal is to bring good-paying jobs to our state and our region, regardless of what the company may be.

Bradley Byrne

President Bush, Secretary of State Rice, and several cabinet level officials have visited Alabama's Gulf Coast in recent days to tour the devastation and to offer their continuing support and prayers for everyone affected by the storm.

Jo Bonner

When states like Alabama and Arizona passed some of the harshest immigration laws in history, my Attorney General took them on in court and we won.

Barack Obama

My uncle is a Southern planter. He's an undertaker in Alabama.

Fred Allen

We must educate and train our children to compete and succeed in the 21st century. Our kids are not going to grow up to compete with children in Alabama or Mississippi. They're going to grow up to compete with kids in India, and China, all over the world; children who are learning to compete and succeed in the 21st century themselves.

Marco Rubio

Captain Richard Phillips of the good ship Maersk Alabama - and Sully Sullenberger splashing down his crippled airliner in the Hudson River - broke through the poisonous smog of economic depression and Wall Street skullduggery with a reminder that pure individual heroism is a daily occurrence if we know where to look for it.

Tina Brown

Ladies and gentlemen: There can be no greater investment in Alabama's future than an investment in education.

Bob Riley

Just think about it: what in the name of God would Alabama be without the University of Alabama? What would Oklahoma be without the University of Oklahoma? Nothing.

Dan Jenkins

For women in, say, Alabama, 'feminism' is a dirty word. They would never march in the streets. But although they don't think of themselves as the beneficiaries of feminism, they are.

Hanna Rosin

Alabama farmers want a chance to complete fairly in Japan, but they can't if the Japanese won't let us in.

Mike Rogers

Most of all, our troops from Alabama said they appreciate the care packages from folks back home.

Mike Rogers

I went to Alabama, so I'm still very devoted to Alabama football and the SEC.

Joe Scarborough

Please know that my thoughts and prayers, as well as those of many, many others here in Alabama and around the country, are with each of you during this time.

Jo Bonner

They would come down in Mississippi, they hired me as a talent scout. And I would go all over Mississippi, Alabama, Texas, and find out different artists for them.

Ike Turner

Alabama citizens, like the vast majority of Americans, respect and value the meaning of decency, and appreciate public institutions that reflect the common values of our society.

Mike Rogers

One thing I've been thinking about is taking the social issues out of national politics. For example, if Georgia wanted abortion and Alabama didn't, that's going to be up to the people in Georgia. I can't sway them. Would I give them advice not to? Absolutely. Would I say it's wrong? Yes.

Joe Wurzelbacher

We hunt in Florida, where I live in Jay. I hunt in Alabama a little bit, on my uncle's land. I go to Illinois and hunt with some friends up there. I hunt in Mississippi and Missouri.

Boo Weekley

All we did in Alabama was have a read through with the script, but there was, 'No, well, it needs more. You've got to do this, Albert. You've got to do that, Jessica.' It didn't feel like that at all.

Albert Finney

My girlfriend and I rented a nice house on the river and I was there for about two and a half months, and we were just out of Alabama. I hardly got to see Alabama.

Albert Finney

Beginning in June, Alabama seniors previously without prescription drug coverage should begin to see savings of between 10 and 25 percent on their medications.

Mike Rogers

The Broadcast Decency Enforcement Act of 2004 helps address the continuing degradation on the broadcast airwaves and helps send a clear message to the broadcast industry that Alabama families, like the rest of American families, have had enough.

Mike Rogers

I had an art teacher who's the reason I got there in high school who encouraged me to go to Alabama. That's where she had gone and kept raving over their art department.

Sela Ward

With 'Selma,' I grew up in Alabama, 45 minutes away from Selma. I have gone to that commemorative march many times with my parents.

Andre Holland

Dixie has just fallen to pieces. There are little patches of Dixie. But even in the heart of Dixie - in Alabama - Dixie is slipping. They've stopped using the word in commercial listings.

John Shelton Reed

We've always been suburb people, and we lived in the East Bay when I was in Oakland. This time around, we're staying in the city, and my kids are getting that city life experience, which is something you don't get too much of in Alabama.

Tim Hudson

I'm always kind of hoping that I'll get a movie that shoots in Alabama so I can go back and kind of get a break from my city life.

Nolan Gould

I grew up in Alabama in a very small town and didn't have access to the finest of anything, really. But my mother was the kind of woman who just wanted us, me and my sisters, to be exposed to any and anything she could find.

Andre Holland

I have this friend who has a theory that lots of towns have energies. And, for instance, certain places in Alabama have bad ones because they were built on reservations or built on cemeteries or something. But Nashville has a really gravitational, magnetic pull.

Caitlin Rose

Pensacola isn't Florida, really. It's the Panhandle. It's right up there near Alabama and Louisiana. It's, like, a stroll away from New Orleans. I feel like New Orleans is home.

Katy Mixon

I think people can learn from my experience - you know, any young people who are under pressure, whether you work on

Wall Street or you work in a factory in Alabama, and young journalists.

Jayson Blair

My mother was from Mississippi, or is from 'Mississippi;' my father was from Alabama. He speaks about conditions in Mississippi and Alabama. They were really the poster children for the bad public laws that segregated, according to race, in our country.

Faye Wattleton

In the state of Alabama we have a significant number of illegal aliens that are leaving our state as occurred in Arizona after they got tough on illegal aliens.

Mo Brooks

I'm in Alabama. First thing I want to say is Roll Tide! I was at the Alabama/Georgia game last year sitting right in the middle of the Alabama section and saw that they rolled all over them!

Brian Jordan

In Israel, if a person doesn't agree with you, she just says no. In Alabama, someone would say, 'I'll think about it.' We would take that literally. So, if you ask for a favor and someone says they'll think about it, they're really not thinking about it.

Odeya Rush

When I moved to Chicago, I was coming from a school that didn't have any arts in Alabama. I essentially came from a town where the arts didn't exist and the desire for education didn't exist and wasn't valued.

Nelsan Ellis

Our original name was Wild Country, but when we first went to The Bowery, they had the name of all 50 states around the edge of the club, so we went to the sign that said 'Alabama' and stuck our band name underneath it.

Randy Owen

The state of Alabama is serious about economic development, and we have shown that the Mobile region has a skilled workforce that is developing every day, strong infrastructure, and an abundance of natural resources.

Bradley Byrne